Visit from an Unknown Woman

Christopher Hampton was born in the Azores in 1946. He wrote his first play, *When Did You Last See My Mother?*, at the age of eighteen. Since then, his plays have included *The Philanthropist, Savages, Tales from Hollywood, Les Liaisons Dangereuses, White Chameleon, The Talking Cure, Appomattox* and *A German Life*. *Appomattox* was turned into an opera by Philip Glass in 2014. He has translated plays by Ibsen, Molière, von Horváth, Chekhov and Yasmina Reza (including *'Art'* and *The God of Carnage*). He has translated seven plays by Florian Zeller, including *The Father* and *The Son*, both of which he subsequently co-wrote for the screen with Florian Zeller, winning an Oscar for Best Adapted Screenplay for *The Father* in 2021. Musicals include *Rebecca, Stephen Ward, Sunset Boulevard* and *The Third Man*. His television work includes adaptations of *The History Man, Hôtel du Lac* and *The Singapore Grip*. His screenplays include *The Honorary Consul, The Good Father, Dangerous Liaisons, Mary Reilly, Total Eclipse, The Quiet American, Atonement, Cheri, A Dangerous Method, Ali & Nino, Carrington, The Secret Agent* and *Imagining Argentina*, the last three of which he also directed.

Stefan Zweig was born in 1881 into an affluent Austrian-Jewish family in Vienna. He was known first as a poet and translator and then as a biographer. He travelled widely in Europe before settling in Salzburg in 1913. In the 1920s and 1930s, he was one of the most widely translated and popular writers in the world. He wrote a string of novellas that were international bestsellers, including *Letter from an Unknown Woman, Fear* and *Amok*. In 1934, driven into exile by the Nazis, he moved to London and became a British citizen. With the fall of France in 1940, Zweig moved to New York before settling in Brazil. In 1942, he and his second wife were found dead in a double suicide.

CHRISTOPHER HAMPTON

Visit from an Unknown Woman

based on the short story by
STEFAN ZWEIG

FABER & FABER

First published in 2024
by Faber and Faber Limited
The Bindery, 51 Hatton Garden, London ECIN 8HN
Typeset by Agnesi Text, Hadleigh, Suffolk
Printed in England by CPI Group (UK) Ltd, Croydon CRO 4YY

Christopher Hampton is hereby identified as author
of this work in accordance with Section 77 of the
Copyright, Designs and Patents Act 1988

A CIP record for this book is available from the British Library

ISBN 978-0-571-39321-3

Printed and bound in the UK on FSC® certified paper in line with our continuing
commitment to ethical business practices, sustainability and the environment.

For further information see faber.co.uk/environmental-policy

1 2 4 6 8 10 9 7 5 3

Characters

Stefan

Marianne

Johann

Young Marianne

Visit from an Unknown Woman, based on the short story by Stefan Zweig, was first performed at Hampstead Theatre, London, on 21 June 2024. The cast was as follows:

Young Marianne Jessie Gattward
Johann Nigel Hastings
Stefan Thomas Levin
Marianne Natalie Simpson

Director Chelsea Walker
Designer Rosanna Vize
Lighting Designer Bethany Gupwell
Sound Designer Peter Rice
Composer Max Perryment
Movement Director Michela Meazza
Casting Director Arthur Carrington

The play was commissioned by the Theater in der Josefstadt, Vienna, where it was first performed (in a translation by Daniel Kehlmann) on 20 March 2020.

Introduction

Christopher Hampton

When I began to study German at school in the early 1960s, the first literary texts we were given to read (on the grounds of their simplicity and lucidity) were Kafka's *The Trial* (from which I later wrote a libretto for Philip Glass) and *Vier Novellen* (Four Short Stories) by Stefan Zweig. *Letter from an Unknown Woman* was not one of the four, but my interest in Zweig was sufficiently piqued to prompt me to seek out some more of his stories. Although at that time Zweig was no longer a fashionable name (he must have been an enthusiasm of my German teacher), I soon discovered that in the 1920s and '30s – not unlike his British contemporary Somerset Maugham – he had been one of most popular and respected authors in the world. Now, like Maugham, his reputation was still overshadowed, not to say tainted, by his extreme bestsellerdom. This was of no interest to me and I continued to read his stories with increasing pleasure and involvement; and the story I found most memorably haunting was this apparently simple tale of a young woman's hopeless love for a commitment-phobic author. Later, I tracked down Max Ophüls's 1948 Hollywood version in one of those decrepit but wonderful London cinemas (now vanished) that showed classic films; and I found it overwhelmingly moving.

I'd had at the back of my mind for some time the idea of dramatising the story for the stage; but it was only when Herbert Föttinger, artistic director of the Theater in der Josef-stadt in Vienna, a theatre with which I've had a long and very fruitful relationship, suggested I might like to adapt something from their local author (Zweig's Vienna apartment is no more than two streets away from the theatre) that the idea became a practical reality. There was some concern about my choice – the story is a monologue in which the shadowy figure of the writer scarcely exists except through the eyes of his worshipper – but once it occurred to me that the writer (known in the story only as R.) might be someone very like Zweig himself – and there are unmistakable autobiographical elements in the story – I was able to persuade Herbert to trust me (given that I have some form in adapting epistolary fiction) to find a workable theatrical structure for the piece.

Zweig wrote the novella in 1922; and Ophüls had moved it back to *c.*1900, to a Vienna of duels and elegance, waltzes and fiacres. I decided, on the contrary, to move the events forward to the 1930s, at a time when Stefan (as I christened the Zweig-like author in the play) could scarcely hope (despite an instinct to bury his head in the sand) to be unaware of the dangers beginning to threaten a Jewish writer in the Vienna of 1934. In this way, I was able to align the play with two other recent pieces of work: *Youth Without God* (also a commission from the Josefstadt theatre) adapted from the novel by Ödön von Horváth; and a monologue, *A German Life*, written for Maggie Smith and inspired by a documentary about one of Goebbels's secretaries, interviewed when she was a hundred and two by a collective of Viennese filmmakers headed by Christian Krönes. Thus, *Visit from an Unknown Woman* is the final panel of an informal triptych, concerning itself principally with life in the German-speaking world between the election of Hitler and the outbreak of the Second World War. It's no doubt unnecessary to explain why, in this age of crude populism, systematic misinformation and irrational enthusiasm for the most obviously inadequate, self-serving and malevolent narcissists available, that particular historical period should tend to prey on one's mind.

VISIT FROM AN UNKNOWN WOMAN

ONE

A comfortable apartment in Vienna, 1934.

At present, the apartment is in darkness; after a moment, the light in the stairwell goes on, illuminating the top of the stairs and a fragment of the landing leading to the front door. Presently, Stefan appears: he's a handsome man of forty, elegantly dressed and groomed, a small, neat moustache and a heavy overcoat flecked with snow. He pauses on the landing and speaks:

Stefan It's this floor.

Marianne appears. She's a very beautiful woman of twenty-eight, tastefully and expensively dressed, but, surprisingly, without a coat or gloves, just a light shawl over the bare shoulders exposed by her evening gown. She pauses for a moment as she arrives on the landing, looks into the darkness to the right, away from Stefan's front door, which he's in the process of unlocking.

Marianne Yes.

Stefan This way.

Inside the door, he turns the light on to reveal a large, well-furnished, book-lined living room, good pictures on the walls, some Far Eastern ornaments and a Roman bust, rugs on the wood floor, a small dining table, a large, untidy writing desk in the window and, near the entrance to the apartment, an occasional table with a blue crystal vase containing white roses. There's a kitchen to one side of the living room and a bedroom leading off the other side. Marianne stands in the doorway taking it all in.

Come in, come in.

She advances a couple of paces, hangs up her shawl on the coatstand.

You must be freezing. Don't you have a coat?

Marianne I left it at the Tabarin.

Stefan Oh.

Marianne My friend, the . . . man I was with, he had the cloakroom tickets. I didn't think it would be very tactful to ask him for mine.

Stefan No, I see. Well, come in and get warm.

Marianne advances into the room, looking around her.

Don't they know you at the Tabarin?

Marianne Not really.

Stefan I hope I haven't got you into trouble.

Marianne It doesn't matter.

There's a kind of weary melancholy in her voice that catches his attention. He crosses to her and takes her in his arms.

Stefan Oh, you are cold.

He looks down at her for a moment, then kisses her on the lips. The response is rather more ardent than he was expecting and when they break apart, he's trying to conceal his pleasure and surprise.

Have you eaten? Would you like something?

Marianne No, I've had dinner, thank you.

Stefan Some champagne, perhaps?

Marianne I've probably had enough.

Stefan smiles and produces a silver cigarette case, which he offers to her. She shakes her head.

I don't smoke.

Stefan Do you mind if I . . .?

Marianne Of course not.

Stefan lights himself a cigarette; then he leads Marianne over to the sofa and, once she's settled, sits next to her. He looks at her for a moment.

Stefan You're very intriguing.

Marianne In what way?

Stefan How's your friend going to react to your going off with a stranger?

Marianne Not very well, I suspect.

Stefan I just thought . . . you know, if I were lucky, that you might agree to give me an address or a telephone number. I never imagined you would leave with me.

Marianne I wanted to.

Stefan Well, I'm very flattered.

Marianne Seemed to me as if it might be something that happened to you quite often.

Stefan No, I assure you.

Marianne The way you looked across at me from your table.

Stefan I was very struck by you. I was wondering why we hadn't run into one another before.

Pause. Marianne's smile is slightly twisted.

Marianne Yes, that is strange.

Stefan You live in Vienna, do you?

Marianne Oh, yes.

Stefan Of course, I travel a lot.

Marianne What . . . do you do?

Stefan I'm a writer.

Marianne Oh? What sort of thing do you write?

Stefan Novels. Biographies. I started out wanting to be a playwright, but . . .

Marianne But what?

Stefan My first two plays, one was set up here, the other in Berlin, both with very famous actors. And they both died during rehearsals, believe it or not. So I thought maybe the theatre was trying to tell me something.

Marianne To write for younger actors, perhaps.

Stefan Yes. Or possibly not to depend on other people.

Silence. Marianne looks around the room. Stefan stubs out his cigarette.

Marianne Beautiful roses.

Stefan Yes. Something of a mystery.

Marianne What do you mean? In what way?

Stefan Every year, on my birthday, somebody sends me a bunch of white roses.

Marianne You don't know who?

Stefan No idea.

Marianne So, is it your birthday?

Stefan Yesterday. I was forty.

Marianne Did you have a big celebration?

Stefan doesn't answer for a moment; he takes her hand.

Stefan No. I was saving that for tonight.

He stands, drawing her up. He leads her towards the bedroom.

Blackout.

TWO

Early the next morning. Stefan's valet, Johann, a dignified figure in his late fifties, is tidying up. He notices Marianne's evening bag on the sofa, doesn't touch it, works around it. Presently, Marianne herself steps into the room, dressed as in the previous scene.

Johann Good morning, miss.

Marianne You must be Johann.

Johann How did you . . . ?

Marianne Stefan mentioned you.

Johann Favourably, I hope.

Marianne Of course. He was saying you'd been with him for nearly twenty years and that he wouldn't know what to do without you.

Johann Well, you can come again.

Marianne looks away; Johann, feeling he may have overstepped the mark, adopts a more formal manner.

Would you prefer tea or coffee, miss?

Marianne Coffee, please.

Johann I'll see to it. Breakfast won't be long.

Marianne I'm not feeling terribly hungry.

Johann I'll prepare a few things, you can help yourself as you . . .

He breaks off, frowning. He's looking at her intently.

Marianne What is it?

Johann Nothing, miss, forgive me, I thought for a moment . . . It's nothing.

*He steps aside into the kitchen, where he can be heard
fetching out plates and cups. Marianne reaches into her
evening bag for some lipstick, which she applies in front
of a small mirror near the front door. As she's completing
this process, Stefan appears, comfortably dressed for his
day's work.*

Stefan Good morning.

Marianne Good morning.

He crosses the room to her.

Stefan I'm sorry you've just done that.

*He's referring to the lipstick, which he smudges with
a kiss.*

Marianne I can always redo it.

Stefan And I can always re-undo it.

*He kisses her again, becoming aware of clatter from
the kitchen.*

You've met Johann?

Marianne Yes, just now.

Stefan I'm sorry, I meant to warn you he came in early.

Marianne He's been with you a while, I imagine.

Stefan Best part of twenty years.

*Johann comes in with cups on a tray: coffee for Marianne,
tea for Stefan. Marianne turns away with her cup, as
Stefan adds milk and a lump of sugar and stirs.*

I like tea the way the English drink it.

Marianne Have you spent a lot of time in England?

Stefan Yes, on and off. I don't like London all that much,
but I'm very partial to Bath.

6

Marianne I've never been.

Johann has been laying the breakfast table; now he heads back towards the kitchen.

Johann Breakfast won't be long.

Stefan moves over to sit at the table; he gestures to Marianne.

Stefan Come.

Marianne I'm not sure I need any breakfast.

Stefan Oh, I do. Come . . .

He breaks off, shakes his head.

I'm very sorry, this is embarrassing, but I'm afraid I didn't catch your name.

Marianne I don't believe I threw it.

She sips her coffee, staying where she is.

I'd better go, I have things to do; and then I should go home, always supposing there is still such a place.

Stefan Do you think he's going to take it that badly?

Marianne I don't know, this hasn't happened before.

Stefan I'm sorry if I . . .

Marianne It was my decision, it's nothing to do with you.

Stefan Well, something, perhaps . . .

Marianne You're not to blame is what I mean.

Stefan I wish I could help. But I'm going away this afternoon.

Marianne Are you?

Stefan Yes, for two or three months. To Morocco. To finish my novel.

Slightly surprisingly, Marianne goes over to sit at the table with Stefan.

Marianne Why can't you finish it here?

Johann appears with breakfast: rolls, rye bread, cheese, ham, charcuterie, butter, jam, fruit. A pause, as he distributes the plates. Stefan reaches for a roll and begins eating as he gives Marianne a thoughtful answer.

Stefan This isn't a particularly easy time to be a Jewish writer. The last thing I did was a libretto for a famous composer. First, he said did I mind if they left my name off the posters? I did mind, although I finally agreed: but they took the opera off after two performances anyway. Because of me. I understand the composer's looking for a different librettist. Can't blame him.

Marianne Why couldn't he have stood up for you?

Stefan He did as much as he felt he could.

Pause. For a moment, he eats thoughtfully.

The thing is, I've never thought of myself as a Jewish writer. I'm not part of Jewish culture, I love Goethe and Rilke, I'm part of German culture. Or I was. Unfortunately, for the time being, there's no such thing.

Silence.

Marianne I'm sorry you're going away.

Stefan Are you? Are you really?

A spasm of what looks like anger crosses Marianne's face. She stands up and looks straight at him. He puts aside his napkin.

Are you all right?

Marianne I was in love with a man once. He was forever going away.

8

They look at each other for a moment.

Stefan We always come back.

Marianne Yes, but by the time you come back, you've forgotten everything.

Stefan stands up, moves around the table and puts his arms around her.

Stefan I'm not going to forget you.

Marianne I have to go.

She goes to get her lipstick from the bag and re-applies it. As she's doing so, she sees, in the mirror, Stefan slipping a handful of banknotes into her bag. She's horrified, controls herself with the utmost difficulty.

Stefan Johann will see you out.

Marianne It's all right.

Stefan calls into the kitchen.

Stefan Johann, our guest is leaving.

Johann emerges from the kitchen.

Marianne No, there's no need to bother.

Johann It's quite all right, miss.

Marianne has snatched up her bag and begins to move confusedly towards the door; then a thought suddenly strikes her.

Marianne Will you give me one of your roses?

Stefan Of course. With pleasure.

He chooses one and hands it to her.

Marianne Are you sure? Maybe they're from someone who loves you.

Stefan It's possible: but, as I told you, I don't know who sends them to me every year. It's part of their charm.

Marianne Could it be someone else you've forgotten?

Stefan I don't think so.

He kisses her lightly on the forehead.

Thank you.

She looks up at him, then turns away abruptly and hurries to the door, where Johann is waiting, having opened the door, with her shawl. As she takes it, she slips the banknotes out of her bag and gives them to him. He looks at her, surprised. As she hurries away and down the stairs, his expression changes. He's remembered who she is.

Blackout.

THREE

Exactly a year later.
It's quite late in the evening. Stefan is sitting at his desk, his pen uncapped, a notebook open in front of him. He's paused in his writing and is lost in thought. The blue vase is empty.
Outside, the light in the stairwell goes on; and, a moment later, Marianne appears. She stops outside the door, raises a hand to press the doorbell, then lets the hand drop to her side. She looks different: a plain overcoat, scarf and gloves – and her expression somehow defeated, a little desperate. The light has gone out of her eyes. She stands, trying to make up her mind.
Unaware of this, Stefan begins to write.
Outside, the stairwell light snaps out. It's this that jolts Marianne into suddenly ringing the doorbell.
Stefan, surprised by the rather shrill sound of the bell, half swivels in his chair. He puts his pen down and glances at his

watch. He's in two minds as to whether to answer the bell. Finally, sighing, he rises to his feet and sets off towards the front door.

At about this time, Marianne decides no one is in and turns away in the dark. By the time Stefan opens the door, she's started down the stairs. Hearing him, she stops and turns back.

Stefan Yes?

Marianne I'm sorry to call on you so late.

Stefan reaches for the timer by the door and switches the light on again. He peers at her for a moment: then his eyes light up.

Stefan Oh, it's you!

Marianne Yes.

Stefan Well, come in, come in.

She comes back to him; and there's an awkward embrace in the doorway. Then she follows him into the flat. He takes her coat and hangs it up, along with her scarf.

It's lucky I'm here. (*A thought strikes him.*) Is this the first time you've . . . ?

Marianne Yes.

Stefan Oh, good. Because I've been away a lot.

He's shown her over to the sofa, where she sits.

Can I get you something to warm you up? Cognac? Schnapps?

Marianne Thank you. Whatever's . . . to hand.

Stefan pours cognac from a decanter into a couple of brandy glasses.

Stefan As a matter of fact, I'm thinking of moving out.

Marianne Oh?

Stefan It's high time.

Marianne You mean because of . . . ?

Stefan Across the way there's this monstrous idiot – this monstrous *elected* idiot – who keeps telling his fellow idiots to throw my books on a bonfire and beat me up in the street. And sooner or later, he's going to step across and simply steal this flat and everything in it.

As he speaks, he's handed her her drink; this time, he doesn't sit next to her. Instead, he draws up a chair and sits at right-angles to her.

Marianne You think that's what's going to happen?

Stefan Almost inevitably.

He takes a thoughtful swig of brandy; then, his mood lifting, he turns to her.

So, I'm very glad you've found me.

Marianne Are you?

Stefan Of course. That was an astonishing night. Don't you think?

Marianne I've never known a man . . . lose himself in the moment the way you do.

Stefan Thank you, that feels like a compliment.

Marianne It is.

Pause.

Stefan It's some time since . . .

Marianne A year.

Stefan If you knew how many times I'd kicked myself for not asking for your address. I was too preoccupied with my trip, the way my book was going and other trivial matters. I never even found out your name.

Marianne Never mind, at least you remembered me.

Stefan What do you mean? How could I possibly not have remembered you?

Marianne You never have before.

Pause. Stefan stares at her, utterly baffled.

Stefan I don't understand.

Marianne No.

Silence. A wave of emotion sweeps over Marianne, and she buries her face in her hands. Stefan gets up, moves to sit next to her and puts his arm around her shoulders.

Stefan Are you all right?

Marianne raises her face from her hands.

Marianne No.

She looks up at him, her face a mask of misery.

My son died.

Stefan straightens up in shock. Inadvertently, he moves away from her.

Stefan Oh, my God . . . I'm so sorry . . . When, I mean . . . ?

Marianne Last night. In the hospital. I was sitting by his bed on a hard chair and I must have drifted off to sleep for a couple of hours. I hadn't slept all week. And when I woke up, he was gone. That poor, sweet child. He was only ten.

Stefan But this is appalling . . .

Marianne He came home on Monday with some kind of flu. The next day, his temperature was really high so I took him to the hospital. They did what they could but whatever it was turned into pneumonia.

He turns back to her, takes her in his arms. She collapses into him and he holds her for a moment. Now the shock is passing, his expression is becoming increasingly bewildered. Marianne controls herself, pulls back and looks up at him.

I'm sorry, but I felt I had to speak to you. I couldn't think who else to turn to, it had to be you. Will you let me explain?

Stefan Of course.

Marianne Why don't you go back and sit over there? It'll help me to stay calm.

He moves back to the chair he positioned. She takes a deep breath.

I shan't take long; and when I'm finished, I think you'll understand why it had to be you.

Stefan Take as long as you like.

Marianne Thank you.

Pause.

We used to be neighbours.

Stefan What? When?

Marianne When you moved into this flat, the year after the war, my mother and I lived next door in Flat 3.

She points towards the front door. Stefan frowns, thinking furiously.

Stefan I don't . . .

Marianne There's no reason why you should remember. I think we only spoke to each other once in two years.

Stefan Ah.

Marianne My father was killed in the war and my mother moved into Flat 3, her widow's pension just about stretched to cover the rent. Your predecessor in this flat was a violent drunk who regularly beat his wife and children – bullies who used to yell obscenities at me in the street: so it was a great relief when the police came and arrested him one day for embezzlement or something, anyway he went to prison and his family moved out; and we were all delighted when the concierge told us a single man, a writer, had taken the flat. That was the first time I heard your name.

Stefan shifts in his chair, not entirely comfortable, takes a mouthful of brandy.

Johann supervised all the painting and redecorating that took place: we liked him, he was very respectful to my mother and very friendly to me. I was there on the day all your furniture arrived – I'd never seen so many books, all beautifully bound, many of them in French and English and other foreign languages I didn't recognise. But I still hadn't set eyes on you. Of course, by then I was intensely curious about you, how old you were, what you might look like – and that night, I dreamt about you.

Stefan Without ever having seen me?

Marianne That's right: in the dream you were an old man with glasses and a long white beard, but very handsome, very *distingué*. You have to remember, I was only thirteen.

Stefan Oh, I see.

Marianne The first couple of days after you moved in, I kept trying to catch a glimpse of you: without success. But on the third day, there you were, bounding up the stairs two at a time, not old at all, but twenty-five, slim, elegant and impossibly good-looking. I don't know how, but the minute I saw you, I instantly understood the two different sides of your nature: the frivolous, pleasure-loving socialite and the uncompromisingly serious, hard-working writer. This profound split in your character is what defines you; and for some strange reason, I immediately recognised its existence and it caused me to become . . . obsessed with you.

Stefan Obsessed?

Marianne Yes: my entire life revolved around you. You were my only interest. I kept watch on all your visitors and noticed how well they illustrated the two sides of your personality: from the Director of the Opera to the girls from the secretarial college; from your fellow writers and artists to the students you liked to go drinking with. And so many women. Soon after you'd moved in, I was on my way to school, when an older woman, heavily veiled, let herself out of here. At first, I was too innocent to understand I was in love with you.

Stefan No, it was just a crush, not the same thing as love.

Marianne You may be right, because I remember the exact moment when I really did fall in love with you: our first meeting.

Stefan When was that?

Marianne It was after school. I was standing outside the door to the building, saying goodbye to one of my schoolfriends, when a car drew up and you emerged and jumped off the running board. I went to open the door for you, but you were in a hurry as usual and we practically collided. You looked at me, smiled with real tenderness and said, very quietly: 'Thank you very much, Fräulein.'

Stefan 'Thank you very much, Fräulein.' Was that all?

Marianne It was enough: from that moment, I was done for, I was yours. Of course, later on I understood the tenderness was a mechanical habit. It's just the way you look at women. It's a look that takes in everything they're wearing and undresses them at the same time. It's the look of a born seducer. I didn't suspect this at the time, of course, I thought the look was just for me; it was like being washed in fire. When you'd gone, my friend asked me who you were. 'Just a neighbour,' I said. 'In that case,' she said, 'why did you go so red?'

Pause.

I've loved you ever since then.

Stefan No, just a minute . . .

Marianne I know a lot of women have told you they love you, I know how spoiled you are. But I can assure you, no one has ever loved you as slavishly and devotedly as I did – and as I still do.

Stefan You were a child!

Marianne Precisely. And there's nothing that compares to the concealed, unnoticed love of a child, nothing as hopeless or submissive – and nothing as passionately observant. Certainly not the love of a mature woman, which is always compromised and conditional, with half an eye on the effect it's having, on other people as well as herself. But I had no one to confide in, no precedents, no advice, no warnings. I slid unsuspectingly into the abyss.

Stefan, looking a little anxious now, brings out his cigarette case and lights a cigarette.

I know I probably ought to be ashamed of these grotesquely exaggerated feelings, but I'm not; my love was passionate, but it was pure. You weren't even aware of my existence, if I passed you on the stairs, I'd run past you with my head down, like someone jumping into a lake to avoid a forest fire. Even so, just in case you noticed, I always covered up the patch in my school tunic with my satchel; I didn't want you to see it and work out how poor we must be.

Silence. Stefan draws on his cigarette, troubled.

Outside the flat, the light goes on in the stairwell; and the thirteen-year-old Marianne appears, as described, her satchel carefully arranged to cover the patch in her tunic. At the top of the stairs, she stops, darts glances to left and right and up the stairs to check the coast is clear. Then she listens outside Stefan's door for a moment and, for a few seconds, greatly daring, tries to look through the keyhole. Then she slips silently away into her mother's flat, disappearing into the dark.

In the evenings, I used to run down into the street three or four times – I invented a list of plausible excuses – so I could tell by your lights whether you were in or not. I couldn't bear it when you went away. I dreaded seeing Johann with your yellow valise. While you were gone, I'd cry myself to sleep every night.

Stefan shakes his head disapprovingly. The light in the stairwell snaps off.

I know. But there were positive aspects to it. You transformed my whole life, in many ways for the better. I'd been bored at school, my marks were below average – suddenly I was top of the class. I started reading every book I could get my hands on, yours of course, which I didn't always understand the first time, but all kinds of other books as well. To my mother's amazement, I even started practising the piano between lessons, because I had a notion that you were fond of music. My mother also couldn't understand why I liked to read sitting on a hard chair in the freezing cold hallway rather than in the living room by the stove.

At the far edge of the stage, lights come up on the thirteen-year-old Marianne, sitting on a hard chair, a book open on her knees.

Stefan And why did you?

18

The light goes on in the stairwell. Immediately, the thirteen-year-old Marianne, throwing a quick glance back towards the living room, jumps to her feet and – keeping her book in one hand as a possible alibi – goes to put her eye against something we can't see.

Marianne We had a small brass spyhole in our front door.

Stefan gives a chuckle of understanding.

Don't laugh! That spyhole was my window on the world. I watched all your friends and lovers come and go and knew enough about them to be able to divide them into those I liked and those I hated. I knew all your clothes, all your suits and ties and, from what you were wearing, I could make a pretty good guess at where you were going and with whom.

Stefan stubs out his cigarette and rises to his feet. Lights snap out on the thirteen-year-old Marianne.

Stefan Yes, but what about your son? I want you to tell me about your son.

Marianne I will, I promise.

Stefan is over by the decanter.

Stefan Another drink?

Marianne No, thank you.

Stefan I think I'll have one.

He pours himself another brandy.

Marianne I want to tell you about the most beautiful experience of my childhood: you're not to laugh.

Stefan Of course not.

Marianne You were away. It was a Sunday, I think, and Johann was taking the opportunity to beat the rugs from here and from your bedroom. When he'd finished, I saw him struggling up the stairs with one and, on an impulse, I went out and offered to help him. He was very glad of a hand and when we'd got the last one up, the one in your bedroom, and he was busy laying it out, I had a chance to spend a couple of minutes in this room, just looking around.

She falls silent. Stefan is still on his feet, his back to the front door, which now, of its own accord, swings open to admit the thirteen-year-old Marianne. Neither of them is aware of her, of course, nor she of them, but she stands for a moment, looking round the room with an expression of awe and reverence. Finally, she picks up the blue crystal vase on the table near the front door and rests it for a moment against her cheek.

I can honestly say those were the happiest few moments of my entire childhood.

The thirteen-year-old Marianne replaces the vase carefully and slips out of the room, the door closing behind her. Stefan, meanwhile, is digesting what Marianne has said.

Stefan I'm sorry. I find that desperately sad.

Marianne No, no, you mustn't. I wish I could find the words to convince you how happy it made me.

Stefan, shaking his head, resumes his seat.

Anyway, I was so obsessed with you, I'd been paying no attention to my mother; I hadn't even noticed this elderly man, an old family friend from Innsbruck, had been calling round more and more frequently. So I was completely taken by surprise when one day my mother summoned me to her room and told me he had proposed to her and she had accepted, principally, she said, for my sake. 'That's fine,' I said, 'as long as it makes you happy.' And then a thought suddenly struck me and I said, 'We won't have to move, will we?' 'Oh, yes,' she said, 'naturally we would have to go and live with Ferdinand in Innsbruck.' It was such a shock, I . . .

Stefan What?

Marianne Apparently I fainted dead away.

Stefan Good God.

Marianne Yes, my mother was extremely alarmed. After that, everything moved very fast. One day I came home from school and all the furniture had gone, except for two camp beds for my mother and me.

Lights up on the thirteen-year-old Marianne, standing in the hallway of her mother's flat, her expression anguished.

It seemed to me I couldn't live without you. And suddenly – my mother had gone out – I decided I had to speak to you.

Looking terrified, the thirteen-year-old Marianne advances towards Stefan's door, where she stands for a moment, paralysed with fear.

I'd no idea what I was going to say to you. All I knew was that I had to see you. Something I couldn't understand, something larger than me, was pushing me forward. I stood there for what felt like an eternity, every terrible second stretching out forever – and then my arm, which seemed to be independent from my body, reached out and rang your bell.

The thirteen-year-old Marianne rings the bell, shrill and loud. No reaction from Stefan or Marianne.

I can hear it now, the piercing sound of that bell and then the blood-freezing silence that followed.

Silence. The thirteen-year-old Marianne waits, shivering with fear.

What was I thinking? I'd probably have fallen on my knees and asked you to take me on as a maid, an unpaid servant. But you were out, of course. And Johann must have been out as well. So there was nothing for me to do but to take the few steps back to our flat, which felt like struggling for hours through deep snow.

The thirteen-year-old Marianne reluctantly makes her way back. Lights out on the landing.

I was still determined to speak to you before I left. There was nothing sexual about it, I was too innocent for anything like that or to understand my real feelings; I just wanted to see you again, hear your voice, cling on to you and never let you go. So I waited for my mother to go to sleep and crept back out into the hall.

The thirteen-year-old Marianne reappears, in her nightdress. In the absence of the hard chair, she lies down on the floor.

It was a bitterly cold January night, but I thought if I put on something warm, I might fall asleep and miss you. I was exhausted, every limb was aching. I was freezing in the icy draught.

As she speaks, the lights on Stefan's flat fade to darkness. Only the thirteen-year-old Marianne, lying shivering on the floor in the dim light can be seen. Marianne's voice continues in the darkness, now on speakers.

(V.O.) I waited almost the whole night. I had to stand up every few minutes, because I kept getting cramp. Finally – it must have been about three in the morning – I heard the key in the lock and . . .

The light in the stairwell snaps on and the thirteen-year-old Marianne scrambles to her feet and steps out on to the landing.

(V.O.) I still had no idea what I was going to do: fall at your feet, throw myself into your arms – I just knew this was my destiny. And then . . .

From the stairwell rises the unmistakable sound of a woman's nervous laughter.

(*V.O.*) You were with a woman.

Suppressing a gasp of horror, the thirteen-year-old Marianne hurries back into the darkness of her mother's flat.

There's a few seconds of hiatus and then a young couple comes into view, reaching the top of the stairs.
It's Stefan and Marianne.

FOUR

It's 1924, which means that Stefan is thirty and Marianne is eighteen.
They're both in a state of heightened excitement: she for obvious reasons and he because, as far as he's concerned, he's on the brink of a new conquest. Marianne is carrying a bunch of white roses.
Stefan, failing to keep his impatience in check, forges ahead of her.

Stefan It's this floor.

Marianne pauses on the landing, looks towards the front door of her old flat.

Marianne Yes.

Stefan This way.

He unlocks the front door and steps into the flat; but instead of switching on the main light, he crosses the room, switches on the lamp on his desk, then moves to turn on the kitchen light: so that the room is lit obliquely, not to say romantically. Then he takes the blue crystal vase, steps into the kitchen and fills it at the sink. Meanwhile Marianne stands in the doorway, holding the flowers.

Marianne These are so beautiful.

Stefan brings back the filled vase, puts it on the table and takes the roses from her.

Stefan Not as beautiful as you.

He arranges the roses carefully in the vase.

This is definitely your flower, don't you think? Much more so than those vulgar red roses he was trying to push on us.

Marianne It will be from now on.

Stefan There. That will keep them fresh for you.

He turns to her. It must be summer, because they're both very lightly dressed. He takes her delicate shawl and hangs it on the coatstand. Then he takes her in his arms and kisses her. Finally, he breaks away.

Champagne?

Marianne I think maybe I've had enough already.

Stefan I'm not sure one can ever have enough champagne. Something else?

Marianne No, thank you, really.

Stefan Well, then, come and sit down.

He leads her over to the sofa, sits down next to her.

I hope you're not going to get into trouble, staying out this late.

Marianne No.

Stefan You're very mysterious. The only thing that wasn't a surprise to me is when you told me you were a model in a showroom.

Marianne It was certainly a surprise to me. I've only been in Vienna a couple of weeks; my parents live in Innsbruck and my stepfather arranged, through old friends of his, a sales job in a fashion house. But as soon as Madame Spitzer, the couturière, set eyes on me, she asked me if I wouldn't prefer to model clothes for the clients.

Stefan A woman of taste. (*Leans in to kiss her; then draws back, anxious not to rush things.*) You must live around here.

Marianne No, I live in Vienna 18.

Stefan But I saw you a couple of days ago, didn't I?

Marianne Yes, that's right, you did.

Stefan That's what gave me the courage to speak to you. I thought perhaps we were neighbours.

Marianne No. We're not neighbours.

Stefan Well, what a piece of luck!

Marianne What?

Stefan That you happened to be passing twice in a week. And you say you've only just arrived in Vienna.

Marianne Yes.

Stefan I call that luck.

Marianne Yes.

Stefan Or destiny.

Marianne Yes.

Stefan If there is such a thing.

Pause. He reaches out to caress her.

Marianne At dinner, you said you were a writer.

Stefan Yes: I've been very spoiled. I'd always wanted to be a writer, but I never expected I'd be able to make a living at it; let alone a good living. But my first book, which was published right before the war, was an instant success. The war itself was an interruption, of course, but luckily for me, I failed a series of medicals and finished up working in the War Archive; not very glorious, but there's no doubt it suited me better than trying to push a bayonet into the guts of some poor wretched Russian peasant.

He reaches round behind her, to begin unbuttoning her dress.

Marianne What are you writing now?

Stefan A biographical sketch of Dostoevsky. Anything not to have to think about this miserable century.

Marianne You think the last century was any better?

Stefan Oh, yes, much.

Marianne Yes, I suppose in this century they actually would have shot Dostoevsky.

Surprised by this remark, Stefan pauses in his task. He looks at her for a moment.

Stefan You're quite a strange girl.

Marianne In what way?

Stefan Well, for one thing, most other girls I know would have at least made a pretence of staving me off.

Marianne I have no intention of staving you off.

Long pause. They look at each other.

Stefan Then shall we . . . move into the other room?

Marianne Let's.

Stefan stands, drawing Marianne up. He leads her towards the bedroom.

Blackout.

Lights up on the stairwell. The thirteen-year-old Marianne, now dressed for travel, comes out of her

mother's flat carrying a suitcase. She hesitates for
a moment, looking longingly at Stefan's door, but
a woman's voice calls brusquely from below: 'Where
are you? Come along!' She tears herself away and
heads reluctantly down the stairs. Over this, we hear
Marianne's voice.

(*V.O.*) When I left my mother's flat for the last time, I could never have imagined that some day I would be one of those women you brought home with you. I was so unhappy those three years in Innsbruck.

FIVE

1935: a continuation of Scene Three. Marianne is on the
sofa, Stefan sits at right-angles to her.
  The vase is empty.

Marianne I behaved very badly; my poor stepfather tried his best to be kind to me, he bought me beautiful clothes, tried to tempt me to concerts and theatres and on trips abroad – but all I wanted to do was stay at home and think about you. Small town, Innsbruck, but I never learned my way around it; I was too busy reliving every single encounter with you and everything I'd witnessed when I had you under surveillance. Of course, whenever you published a new book, I devoured it – and any day your name appeared in the newspapers, which was quite often, was a red-letter day for me. I checked the Vienna papers regularly to decide which concerts or first nights might interest you – and then I imagined you walking into the theatre and greeting your friends or taking your subscription seat in the concert hall. And as I grew older, I began to fantasise about you in a different way, I began to think about making love with you. As soon as I turned eighteen, I started badgering my stepfather about coming back to Vienna, about earning my own living. All he wanted was to support me in style until

he found someone suitable for me to marry, but he didn't
stand a chance. I was so uncompromisingly obstinate,
that he finally gave in and arranged this job for me at the
fashion house. You know what I did when I finally arrived
in Vienna? I put my suitcases into Left Luggage, jumped on
a tram and came straight here. And you were in, your light
was on! I stood below in the street and told myself that now
there was only a windowpane between us, but of course
I was no closer to you than I had been in Innsbruck. Still,
I stood there until your light went out.

A slight groan from Stefan.

I got off work at six o'clock every evening; and as soon as
they rolled down the shutters, I was on my way here. I told
myself it was only a matter of time. I saw you crossing the
street one evening, but when you glanced at me, I lowered
my head and ran away. Another time you were with a
woman; and I was so upset I went back to my lodgings,
cried myself to sleep and didn't come back the next
evening.

Finally, you noticed me. We passed quite close to each
other on those narrow Josefstadt pavements and you caught
my eye for a couple of seconds and then – when I couldn't
resist turning back to look at you, I found you were doing
the same. You were interested, I could see that, but, just as
obviously, you had no idea who I was, you didn't begin to
recognise me.

It was strange, I had often tried to be realistic with myself
and acknowledged you might have any number of reasons
to reject me: but it never crossed my mind, for some reason,
that you'd never even noticed me. You see, because I was so
obsessed with you, I couldn't imagine that you'd never even
given me a thought. Understanding that was like a bucket of
cold water in the face.

All the same, I persisted; and a couple of days later, when
we passed each other again, you smiled at me – and then
you turned and caught me up. You spoke to me in that easy,

charming way of yours, walked with me to the end of the street and then invited me for dinner.

You won't remember the little Italian restaurant you took me to – or the evening which must have been like so many other evenings you spent with other women. But to my immense relief, you turned out to be entirely sympathetic and treated me like an old friend, you were gentle and sensitive, not for a second did you try to force yourself on me. I hardly said a word; I was just happy listening to you and being with you.

It was late when we left the restaurant; and as we came out on to the street, you asked me if I still had some time to spare. Then you brought me back here. On the way, you bought me some white roses.

Silence.

Stefan It's an extraordinary story; I've never heard anything like it.

Marianne You never suspected, did you, my darling, that before that night no man had even so much as seen my body? I did everything I could to stop you from guessing and I don't think you . . . felt any kind of resistance.

Stefan But . . . why didn't you tell me who you were?

Marianne I didn't want to frighten you off and . . . I kept hoping you'd remember me. Which was stupid, because when you smiled at me in the street, as I said, there wasn't a flicker of recognition. This evening is the first time you've ever recognised me.

Stefan It somehow makes me feel I took advantage of you.

Marianne No, no, it was the other way round. I threw myself at you. And I'll always be grateful to you, it was the most wonderful night. I've never regretted it, never for a second. And when you were asleep and I was lying beside you, listening to you breathing, I was so happy I lay there all night, weeping in the dark.

Stefan As happy as that.

Marianne Yes, it was the happiest I've ever been in my life.

Stefan My God.

He lights another cigarette, a little shakily.

Marianne I got up very early the next morning, I had to get to work: I took the white roses and left. You had invited me to come back that evening and again for a third night: when you told me you had to go abroad for a couple of weeks. You asked for my address and for some reason – I'd already given you a false name – I asked you to contact me via poste restante. You promised to get in touch the moment you got back.

Pause.

Stefan And did I?

Marianne Of course you didn't. I went to the post office every day for a month, but . . . never once, not a line. I'm not complaining. That's your character: impulsive and forgetful, affectionate and unfaithful. That's the man I fell in love with, so it wouldn't be logical to complain, would it?

Silence. Stefan draws on his cigarette, eyes lowered.

I told you my boy died last night. Of course he was your son as well.

Stefan What?

This hadn't occurred to him: he seems genuinely stunned.

Marianne Yes, he was conceived on one of those three nights.

Stefan But . . .

Marianne I've just told you you were my first lover; and there was no one else from that time to the day he was born.

Stefan Why on earth didn't you tell me?

Marianne I didn't think you'd believe me. A stranger who picked you up in the street? I'm sure you would have reacted generously, certainly given me money, but would you have been able to believe it was your child I was carrying?

Stefan I don't know, I . . .

Marianne Would you have been able to shake off the suspicion that I'd only come to you because you were rich? There would have been a shadow between us.

Stefan I hope I would have trusted you.

Marianne Well, even if that's true, I wouldn't have wanted to do that to you. You need your freedom and your irresponsibility, I could see you had no wish to have a woman and child depending on you. You would have finished up hating me.

Stefan No!

Marianne Not all the time, perhaps, but every now and then, just for a moment, just for an hour. I didn't want to risk that. I wanted to be the only one of your women you would always think of gratefully and lovingly. Of course, I hadn't bargained for the fact that you would completely forget me and never think of me at all.

Silence.

Stefan I don't know what to say.

Marianne I'm sorry, I didn't mean to sound bitter. I know you're a generous man. When I was a child, I often watched you giving money to beggars; but I also noticed you were very pleased to see the back of them.

Stefan I can't deny it.

Marianne The other thing was, I was afraid you'd try to persuade me to have an abortion. That was the last thing

I wanted. Right from the start, that child meant everything to me. But I knew if you said you didn't want it, I wouldn't have known how to say no to you.

Stefan You were hardly more than a child yourself; why were you so determined to have the baby?

Marianne It was yours.

Stefan doesn't know what to say.

It was you. Not elusive and forever slipping out of my grasp, but trapped inside my body and a part of my life forever – or so I thought. You can't imagine how happy that made me feel.

Stefan I . . .

Marianne Of course, there were great difficulties as well. As soon as I started to show, I lost my job and I couldn't go back to Innsbruck or ask my mother for help, she would have been completely appalled. I lived on my savings for a while, but then, in the last month, all my cash was stolen from my room and I had no choice but to go to the labour ward in the public hospital. It was a deathly place, stinking of chloroform and blood.

Stefan Why didn't you tell me, you didn't have to go through that!

Marianne It's probably good that I did. Nowadays, when I read the word 'hell', I know what it means.

Stefan I'm sorry, I'm so sorry.

Marianne Don't be. It's not at all your fault, I've never blamed you for what happened. Not for a moment. And, in one way, giving birth in those squalid conditions taught me a useful lesson.

Stefan What?

Marianne I realised I didn't want to bring up your son in poverty. He should at least be able to live in the same world as you. So . . .

Stefan What did you do? How did you . . . ?

Pause.

Marianne I sold myself.

Stefan You mean . . . ?

Marianne I wasn't exactly a prostitute, I was . . . I think the polite word for it is 'courtesan'. My clients were all quite rich. You'd be surprised how easy it is. I had the looks for it – and once I'd found that first client, one thing led very easily to another.

Stefan This is terrible.

Marianne No, no, your son was a very happy child; and that was the most important thing. People loved him, he was so attractive, women would stop to tousle his hair on the beach in Italy, he looked so dashing on the slopes at Semmering. One of my clients, a count, used his influence to get him into the Theresianum and you can't imagine how handsome he looked in his school uniform. He was like you, he had that same mixture of playfulness and seriousness, he loved books, he made everybody laugh, he spoke perfect French – and the more like you he became, the more I loved him.

Stefan But you had to sell yourself . . .

Marianne It was really no sacrifice. As far as I was concerned, my body belonged to you; and if you didn't want it, I really didn't mind what became of it. My clients were mostly very kind and respectful; if they weren't, I didn't see them again. The count, in particular, kept asking me to marry him: I could have been a countess with a castle in the Tyrol.

Stefan Why did you turn him down?

Marianne I wanted to keep myself free for you.

Stefan But you didn't tell me. How was I supposed
to know?

Marianne I do regret not letting you meet our son, you
would have loved him. But I thought I had to make a choice.
Between you, who were not part of my life and quite happy
not to be, and him, who was part of my life and needed
me for everything. There was only one way I could stay
connected with you.

Silence.

Stefan The white roses.

Marianne That's right. Every year, on your birthday, I sent
you a bunch of white roses.

Stefan So it was you.

Marianne Except for yesterday. I didn't send you any
yesterday, because our son was dying.

Long silence. Stefan is overcome.

From time to time over the years, one of my clients would
say hello to you. When that happened, you would glance
at me appreciatively, but you'd never recognise me or
connect me with the shy girl in your dark bedroom. It was
unbelievably painful. One night, at the opera, I found we
were sitting next to one another in adjacent boxes. All
through the first act, your hand was resting on the velvet
partition between the boxes – and I was longing to lean
forward and kiss it. I had to force myself not to; and at the
first interval I had to ask my companion to take me away,
I couldn't bear to stay.

Stefan You're right, this is becoming more and more
painful.

Marianne Forgive me for speaking about these things; I'll never do it again. And I don't suppose I would ever have told you any of this had we not run into each other last year at the Tabarin.

Pause.

Stefan The man you were with that night, was he one of your . . . clients?

Marianne Not exactly. It had gone beyond that. I was living with him and I'd decided not to see anyone else. He was a kind, generous man, owned factories in Brünn, and he also wanted me to marry him, but I refused him, without giving it a second thought.

Stefan And did he take you back?

Marianne No.

Stefan Oh, I'm sorry.

Marianne It's the only time I ever saw him angry.

Stefan For some reason, I feel particularly bad about this.

Marianne I'd been thinking about you even more than usual; the day before I'd sent you the roses for your birthday: and when I saw you, it seemed like an omen – I mean, I'd suggested the Tabarin, although I normally hate that kind of place. When I saw you, my heart froze. You kept looking at me; your expression was becoming more and more ardent; and when you finally discreetly signalled to me, I knew I would have to follow you out. For one delirious moment, I thought you might have recognised me, but the minute I joined you, I could see you had no idea who I was.

Stefan This is too . . .

He breaks off and buries his face in his hands. Silence. Then Marianne rises to her feet and stretches out a hand.

Marianne Come.

Stefan looks up at her; he's been struggling with his emotions, but now there's a touch of incredulity in his expression.

Stefan You mean . . . ?

Marianne It'll be good for us both.

Stefan Oh. Oh, no . . .

Marianne Why not?

Stefan I'm not even sure I could . . .

Marianne Why not?

Stefan Well, it was different last year, when I thought you were . . .

Marianne . . . a prostitute.

Stefan You know what I mean. Now, after all this . . .

Marianne I'll help you.

He looks up at her. Her hand is still outstretched to him. He doesn't move.
   Pause.

I'll help you. Let me help you.

She leans in to take his hand; he stands up and allows himself to be led away to the bedroom.

Blackout.

A hiatus. Music. Then Marianne, fully dressed, creeps out of the bedroom in the dark. She's holding an unsealed envelope, which she places carefully on the occasional table, resting it against the empty vase. Then she collects her coat and scarf, slips out on to the landing and disappears.

Another pause. Dawn breaks.

36

*Stefan suddenly bursts into the room. He's in his
dressing-gown. He stands, looking around him a little
wildly; then he sees the envelope and hurries over to get it,
returns to the sofa, opens it. A photo falls out; he picks it up,
looks at it and gasps. Then he starts to read.*

Marianne (*V.O.*) By the time you read this, I shall be dead.

*Stefan looks up, panic in his eyes. Then he looks down
again, begins to read out loud.*

Stefan 'I got up in the middle of the night, when you were
sound asleep, wrote this and left. So with any luck, when
you find it, I'll have been gone for several hours, easily long
enough to carry out my plan. My child is gone to me and
you were never really there.'

Marianne (*V.O.*) It's time for me to move on, back into
silence. You may see something about me in the *Freie Presse*
– or not, if I do my job properly. If you do, it will be the last
you will ever hear of me. Dying will be very easy for me,
I assure you. Thank you.

Stefan 'In spite of everything, I'll always be grateful to you.
I hope you have some inkling of how much I loved you.'

Marianne (*V.O.*) I have only one final request: please, my
darling, will you buy some white roses every year on your
birthday and think of me for a moment?

*Johann appears at the top of the stairs and lets himself
into the flat; he's immediately aware that it's not as it
should be. Stefan looks up from the letter in an obvious
state of distress. Johann waits a moment before speaking.*

Johann Are you all right, sir?

Stefan Ah, Johann, did you pass a woman on your way into
the building?

Johann No. Should I have?

Stefan She's been here before, about a year ago. She actually used to live across the hallway, when she was a child.

Johann Yes, I remember her.

A thought strikes Stefan.

Stefan Does that mean you recognised her when she was here last year?

Johann Oh, yes, sir.

Stefan Why didn't you mention it to me?

Johann spreads his hands eloquently.

Listen, I want you to go and get me a copy of the *Freie Presse*. No. Forget that. It's too soon for it to be in the newspapers. Just . . . just buy me a bunch of white roses, would you?

Johann Before breakfast, sir?

Stefan Yes, before breakfast.

Johann Very well, sir.

He turns to leave and is almost at the door when Stefan speaks.

Stefan Johann.

Johann Yes, sir.

Stefan I've been meaning to ask you this for some time; this is probably as good a time as ever. Would you ever consider leaving Vienna?

Johann Leaving? For good?

Stefan I don't have to tell you the way things have been for me lately. I don't know how much longer I can stay in this country. How long I can put up with these morons. And, more to the point, how much longer they can put up with me. I can't help thinking I'd be safer and more comfortable in Paris or London. Or even further afield. New York or even . . . South America.

Johann I see.

Stefan Or perhaps it would be simpler to follow in the footsteps of the little girl from across the hallway.

Johann Now you've lost me, sir.

Stefan I'm sorry, Johann, I thought I'd better put this to you. I think I know what your answer will be, but I wanted you to know you're always welcome to stay with me if I decide to leave the country.

Johann Thank you, sir, I appreciate it.

Pause.

I'll go and get the roses.

He leaves. Stefan stays where he is, the letter in one hand, the photo in the other. After a time, Marianne's voice.

Marianne (*V.O.*) Thank you again, my darling, for everything. I love you. I love you. Goodbye. Marianne.

As she speaks, the thirteen-year-old Marianne appears on the landing outside. Just as before, the front door swings open and the thirteen-year-old Marianne advances into the room. Stefan looks up from the letter.

Stefan Marianne.

The thirteen-year-old Marianne stands watching Stefan. He's looking straight at her, but he doesn't see her.